GW01117266

EXPLORING

EXPLORING

by

JIM COTTER

✜

CAIRNS PUBLICATIONS
HARLECH
2004

© Jim Cotter 2004

Cairns Publications
Dwylan
Stryd Fawr
Harlech
Gwynedd
LL46 2YA

www.cottercairns.co.uk
office@cottercairns.co.uk

ISBN 1 870652 43 6

Typeset in Enschedé 'Renard'
by Strathmore Publishing Services, London EC1

Printed by Stanley Hunt Ltd, Rushden, Northamptonshire
on Colorit Vanilla Offset

CONTENTS

Ten Invitations
   modelled on the Ten Commandments — 1

Five Commandments of Jesus
   Gospel commandments to love — 11

Six Mysteries
   On the character of God — 12

Three Covenants
   Of God, with God, of friendship — 18

Three Promises
   The spiritual values of solitude, simplicity, and silence — 21

Four Blights and Blessings
   The uncompromising version of the Beatitudes according to Luke — 24

Eight Blights and Blessings
   The spiritualized version of the Beatitudes according to Matthew — 28

Five Unfoldings of the Way of Love — 36

Seven Directions of Prayer — 43

From Seven Sins to Seven Virtues — 44

Nine ways of Being Fools for Christ's Sake — 45

Seven Words through the Worst of Times — 46

An Eleventh Commandment — 53

For
Aled
Carol
Geoffrey
and John

for their encouragement
of an exploration

BIBLICAL REFERENCES

p. 11	John 15.10; 15.12-13; Luke 6.27; Mark 12.31; 12.30, paraphrased
pp. 24-27	Based on Luke 6.20-25, and owing much to suggestions of John Dominic Crossan
pp. 28-35	Based on Matthew 5.3-10
p. 36	1 Corinthians 13.4-8, paraphrased
p. 37	Luke 6.27-28, 35-38
p. 42	Ephesians 3.16-19
p. 46	Luke 23.34
p. 47	Luke 23.43
p. 48	John 19.27
p. 49	Matthew 27.46, Mark 15.34
p. 50	John 19.28
p. 51	John 19.30
p. 52	Luke 23.46

For
pondering
mulling
chewing
delving

Read
mark
learn
and
inwardly digest

Ten invitations
I

Be loyal to the will of the One
  who draws you by a still small voice.
Prepare to listen by clearing your life of
  noise and clutter.
Ask yourself what is your deepest desire.

Ten invitations
II

Do not give ultimate loyalty to anything
  but the mysterious divine Creator-Lover.
Live simply and generously
  where greed and addiction rule.

Ten invitations
III

Pay close attention simply to what is.
Ask the questions that arise from such
  contemplation,
and seek to respond in truth.

Ten invitations
IV

Be thankful for small deeds of kindness
   as well as for greater blessings,
and allow the spirit of gratitude
   to melt the ice of fear and pain.
Take time out of time –
   to rest and to be,
   to celebrate and to laugh.

Ten invitations
V

Live steadfastly into the commitments
 you have made.
Face illusion and betrayal with truth
 and courage.
Delve ever deeper into the mines of trust,
 forgiveness, and compassion.

Ten invitations
VI

Welcome both neighbour and stranger
  as human beings to be accepted and valued
  in the same way as you yourself would wish
  to be received.

Ten invitations
VII

Make your contribution to the common good
  of your own country, and of the one world,
  of which you are a citizen.
Reverence the earth
  and replenish what you have taken.

Ten invitations
VIII

Open your heart to kindness and compassion,
  for yourself and for others.
Respond to the lonely with care and tact.
Cast out fear by the gentle persistence
  of prayerful and thoughtful affection.
Share the pain of those whose stories reveal
  harm and shame,
and be with them without intrusion or
  possession.

Ten invitations
IX

Refuse to act on feelings of superiority.
Shun slogans.
Bear the discomfort of what is unresolved.
Listen silently to those who are different from
  yourself,
without anxiety or hurry,
and so avoid the strident claims of the fanatic
  and the self-righteous.
Remember that each of us is contained
  within a whole that is greater than the sum
  of the parts.

Ten invitations
X

Be expectant of the future,
  in faith and hope,
trusting that it will bring gifts beyond anything
  you could predict or imagine.

Five commandments of Jesus

Abide in my love.
Love one another, as I have loved you:
you can have no greater love than this,
  than to lay down your life for your friends.
Love your enemies.
Love your neighbour as yourself.
Above all,
  love God with the whole of your being.

Six mysteries
I Holiness

A Presence,
the Living Mysterious One:
a holy presence,
showing us the wasteland of our wandering,
facing us with our failures to love and be loved,
uncovering the layers of our illusions,
piercing us with the sword that heals,
embracing us with a purging fire,
refusing to let us go.
In the presence of the Holy One,
we tremble.

Six mysteries
II Forgiveness

A Presence,
the Living Mysterious One:
a forgiving presence,
pouring out lifeblood in love for us,
pursuing us and disturbing us
  and accepting us,
taking to heart our wickedness and pain,
a giving that endures whatever the cost,
dissolving evil with the goodness of love.
In the presence of the Forgiving One,
we contemplate.

Six mysteries
III Mercy

A Presence,
the Living Mysterious One:
a merciful presence,
an exchange of love that enriches both,
blessing us abundantly,
filling us with gratitude,
sowing in us seeds of new life,
shaping us for glory.
In the presence of the Merciful One,
we are thankful.

Six mysteries
IV Love

A Presence,
the Living Mysterious One:
a loving presence,
transfiguring our disfigured faces,
striving with our resistant clay,
bringing harmony out of our chaos.
In the presence of the Loving One,
we adore.

Six mysteries
V Healing

A Presence,
the Living Mysterious One:
a healing presence,
listening with us
   to the sound of running water,
sitting with us
   under the shade of the trees of our healing,
walking once more with us
   in the garden in the cool of the day,
anointing us with the oil
   that penetrates the cells of our being,
touching us with steady hands
   to give us courage on our journey.
In the presence of the Healing One,
we rest.

Six mysteries
VI Joy

A Presence,
the Living Mysterious One:
a joyful presence,
running to meet us like a welcoming friend,
laughing with us in the merriment of heaven,
feasting with us at the great banquet,
Clown of clowns,
Fool of fools,
the only Entertainer of jesters.
In the presence of the Joyful One,
we rejoice.

Three covenants
I The covenant of God

I Who Am and Who Shall Be,
I Who Shall Be There For You
in the unpredictable encounter
where For You I Shall Be There,
Life-giving Spirit within you,
Pain-bearing Presence among you,
Love-making Future beyond you,
I call you into being,
and I bind myself to you.
By my own name and nature,
in every eternal moment,
I affirm and renew my covenant,
I fulfil my promise
to love you to glory for ever,
to honour you as my dwelling-place,
and to be loyal to you,
and full of faith in you,
our life-day long.
Amen. So be it.

Three covenants
II A covenant with God

Beloved and faithful Creator,
Life-giving Spirit within each one of us,
Pain-bearing Presence among us,
Love-making Future beyond us,
of my own free will
I choose to share my life with you.
I affirm and renew my covenant,
this day and all my days.
I fulfil my promise
to love you in friendship for ever,
to honour you as my dwelling-place,
and to be loyal to you,
and full of faith in you,
my life-day long.
Amen. So be it.

Three covenants
III A covenant of friendship

In the wonderful Mystery of God,
Life-giving Spirit within you and within me,
Pain-bearing Presence between us,
Love-making Future beyond us,
you have been given to me,
to be cherished in a covenant of friendship.
By my own free will and destiny
I choose to share my life with you.
With and in that greater Love
I promise to do all that I can for your
  well-being for ever,
to honour you as God's dwelling-place,
and to be loyal to you,
and full of faith in you,
our life-day long.
Amen. So be it.

Three promises
I Solitude

Solitude and solidarity:
it is the ancient path of 'chastity',
of affection and goodwill.
Love's promise, love's narrow way.
A way of hope, to be taken to heart,
to be lived from the heart.
The gentle but firm laying aside of 'lust'
the battering of force,
the temptation to dominate by physical power,
the craving for control.
Loneliness is the narrow gate,
the heart's hollowing,
letting others be:
only then do we come to the place
of solitude and solidarity,
of deep communion and love.

Three promises
II Simplicity

Simplicity and spaciousness:
it is the ancient path of 'poverty',
of nakedness and generosity.
Freedom's promise, freedom's narrow way.
A way of hope, to be taken to heart,
to be lived from the heart.
The gentle but firm laying aside of 'rust' –
the cluttering of things,
the temptation to dominate by the power
  of money,
the craving for comfort.
Constriction is the narrow gate,
the heart's hollowing,
letting possessions be:
only then do we come to the place
of simplicity and spaciousness,
of glad conviviality and freedom.

Three promises
III Silence

Silence and stillness:
it is the ancient path of 'obedience',
of listening and truthfulness.
Wisdom's promise, wisdom's narrow way.
A way of hope, to be taken to heart,
to be lived from the heart.
The gentle but firm laying aside of 'fuss'
the clattering of noise,
the temptation to dominate by the power
  of words,
the craving for certainty.
Not knowing is the narrow gate,
the heart's hollowing,
letting words be:
only then do we come to the place
of silence and stillness,
of true conversation and wisdom.

Four blights and blessings
I Destitution

BLESSED ARE YOU POOR,
FOR YOURS IS THE KINGDOM OF GOD.

We are blighted if we are wealthy:
how can we avoid contempt for the poor?

We are blessed if we are destitute
  and homeless:
we are not to be blamed;
we are already in God's domain.

Four blights and blessings
II Starvation

BLESSED ARE YOU THAT HUNGER NOW,
FOR YOU SHALL BE SATISFIED.

We are blighted if we are overfed:
how can we avoid hardness of heart?

We are blessed if we are starving
 and have to beg for food:
we are not at fault;
we will be satisfied.

Four blights and blessings
III Devastation

BLESSED ARE YOU THAT WEEP NOW,
FOR YOU SHALL LAUGH.

We are blighted if we are sleek:
how can we avoid being scornful?

We are blessed if we are downtrodden
  and gaunt with grief:
we are not guilty;
we will laugh for joy.

Four blights and blessings
IV Persecution

BLESSED ARE YOU THAT ARE REVILED NOW,
FOR YOUR REWARD SHALL BE GREAT.

We are blighted if we are successful:
how can we avoid being arrogant
  and disdainful?

We are blessed if we are despised,
  persecuted, mocked, stigmatized:
we are not to be ashamed:
we are well loved and will be honoured.

Eight blights and blessings
I Poverty

BLESSED ARE THE POOR IN SPIRIT:
THEY ARE CITIZENS OF GOD'S DOMAIN.

We are blighted
when we crave more and more possessions:
we are crushed by the weight and burden
   of them.

We are blessed
when we are ready to do without,
to be empty, to be nothing,
to be humble and open to receive,
knowing our need of God:
we have found the secret of living,
and are rich indeed.

Eight blights and blessings
II Grief

BLESSED ARE THOSE WHO MOURN:
THEY WILL FIND CONSOLATION.

We are blighted
when we wallow in self-pity:
we sink into bitterness and despair.

We are blessed
when we accept our experience of sorrow:
we grow in courage and compassion.

Eight blights and blessings
III Insecurity

BLESSED ARE THE GENTLE:
THEY WILL INHERIT THE EARTH.

We are blighted
when, in our insecurity,
we look anxiously for appreciation
　from others:
we claim everything for ourselves,
and yet possess nothing,
wandering unhappily,
and belonging nowhere.

We are blessed
when we accept our insecurity,
and are content to go unrecognized
　and unrewarded,
claiming nothing for ourselves:
the freedom of the earth is ours;
never exiled, we are everywhere at home.

Eight blights and blessings
IV Struggle

BLESSED ARE THOSE
  WHO YEARN FOR JUSTICE TO PREVAIL:
THEY WILL BE SATISFIED.

We are blighted
when we cease to care and be disturbed,
and find ourselves too much at ease:
we are bored,
and disintegrate into dust.

We are blessed
when we hunger, thirst, and strive
for what is just and good:
we are made whole and are well content.

Eight blights and blessings
V Love

BLESSED ARE THE MERCIFUL:
MERCY WILL BE SHOWN TO THEM.

We are blighted
when we show no compassion,
and are insensitive to the needs of others:
we complain of being misunderstood
and are never loved.

We are blessed
when we accept and forgive those who
 harm us:
we find understanding and love.

Eight blights and blessings
VI Truth

BLESSED ARE THE PURE IN HEART:
THEY WILL SEE GOD.

We are blighted
when we live in illusion and fantasy:
we are utterly lost.

We are blessed
when we are honest with ourselves,
when we are refined and chastened,
and seek to live the truth:
we know ourselves and we know God.

Eight blights and blessings
VII Peace

BLESSED ARE THE PEACEMAKERS:
THEY WILL BE CALLED
   THE DAUGHTERS AND THE SONS OF GOD.

We are blighted
when we are at war with ourselves,
when we spread evil and division and hatred,
seeking to dominate others:
we breed our own downfall,
and we never know trust and friendship.

We are blessed
when we create reconciliation and
   goodwill wherever we go,
returning good for evil:
we are indeed the friends of God.

Eight blights and blessings
VIII Life

BLESSED ARE THE PERSECUTED
  FOR THE CAUSE OF JUSTICE:
THEIRS IS THE FREEDOM OF THE CITY OF GOD.

We are blighted
when our lives are shallow and full of fear,
so that we cannot respond in truth when
  we are challenged:
we freeze in death.

We are blessed
when we shed our pettiness,
and know the deep things of God and of
  ourselves,
and so persevere at whatever the cost –
insult, slander, exile, death:
we have life, and know it abundantly.

Five unfoldings of the way of love
I Love's persistence

Love is patient and kind and knows no envy.
Love never clings,
   is never boastful, conceited, or rude.
Love is never selfish,
   never insists on its own way.
Love is not quick to take offence.
Love keeps no score of wrongs,
   nor gloats over the sins of others.
Love rejoices in the truth.
Love is tough:
   there is nothing that it cannot face.
Love never loses trust
   in human beings or in God.
Love never loses hope, never loses heart.
Love still stands when all else has fallen.

Five unfoldings of the way of love
II The gospel way

Love your enemies.
Do good to those who hate you.
Bless those who curse you.
Pray for those who abuse you.
Do good and lend,
   expecting nothing in return.
For God is kind to the ungrateful and selfish.
Be merciful,
   as God, like a good father, is merciful.
Do not judge,
   and you will not be judged.
Do not condemn,
   and you will not be condemned.
Forgive, and you will be forgiven.
Give, and it will be given to you.
The measure you give
   will be the measure you receive.

Five unfoldings of the way of love
III Dwelling in love

If you dwell in the divine love,
if you join the dance of the Lover,
   the Beloved, and the Mutual Friend...
if you are caught up in the love
   that is generous and overflowing...
you will find yourself loving and being loved
   with the whole of your being...
loving your neighbour as yourself,
and loving even your enemy...
and, as surely as night follows day,
you will never use force –
though you will refuse
   to let others escape from love and truth...

you will never use others
   merely to provide what you want –
though you will acknowledge and respect
   your own needs...
you will never take advantage
   of others' ignorance or immaturity –
though you will try to increase
   their knowledge and wisdom.

Five unfoldings of the way of love
IV Love your enemies

Neither condemn nor destroy your enemies.
Keep in 'con-tact' with them –
   even when you cannot keep 'in touch'.
Strive powerfully with them,
   shoulder to shoulder,
   until you see each other face to face.
Be angry, but with compassion, not with hatred.
Do not yield to fury,
   nor to the resentment that leads to bitterness.
Be strongly and persuasively gentle –
   with others and with yourself.
Where there is ice in your heart
   let it be melted by goodwill.

Do not meet oppression with violation –
  we have all been too much hurt.
Your enemies are human beings like yourself:
do not picture them as subhuman,
  dismissed by an insult.
Keep a sense of proportion –
  and a sense of humour.
With an expanding heart, love your enemies.

Five unfoldings of the way of love
V Rooted in love

According to the riches of God's glory
may we be strengthened with power
through the Spirit in our inner being,
and may Christ dwell in our hearts
  through faith,
that being rooted and grounded in love,
we may have power to comprehend
  with all the saints
the breadth and length
  and height and depth of love,
and to know the love of Christ
  which passes knowledge,
that we may be filled with the abundant life
  of God.

Seven directions of prayer

Reaching downwards and delving,
  we are rooted in our true ground.
Reaching upwards and yearning,
  we adore the One who is beyond us.
Being slimmed by admitting the truth,
  we enter life by a narrow gate.
In opening our arms to our neighbour,
  we forgive to seventy times seven.
Reaching backwards into the past,
  we absorb what is good and are thankful.
Reaching forwards into the future,
  we give of ourselves in trust.
Becoming still in the present,
  we rest in the silence of being.

From seven sins to seven virtues

Puncture my bloated pride:
  sow the hidden seed of humility.
Root out my cruel and bitter anger:
  sow the hidden seed of courtesy.
Disentangle me from the web of envy:
  sow the hidden seed of justice.
Make clear the hypocrisies of my lust:
  sow the hidden seed of truth.
Ease my grip from money:
  sow the hidden seed of generosity.
Still my gluttonous pursuit of pleasure:
  sow the hidden seed of charity.
Penetrate the fog of my sloth:
  sow the hidden seed of laughter.

Nine ways of being Fools for Christ's sake

In facing the truth,
  may we be set free from illusion.
In accepting our wounds,
  may we be healed if not cured.
In embracing the outcast,
  may we know ourselves redeemed.
In discovering our inner child,
  may we grow to full stature.
In seeking true innocence,
  may we no longer harm.
In yielding to dying,
  may abundant life flow through us.
In vulnerable risk,
  may we know love's pain and joy.
In the release of laughter,
  may we hear the chuckle of God.
In the folly of the Cross,
  may we see the Wisdom of God.

Seven words

I

In the story of the crucifixion,
Jesus prayed for the soldiers who crucified him,
that they might be forgiven.

The Love of God always sees far with
  compassion.

Seven words
II

In the story of the crucifixion,
Jesus welcomed the penitent thief
  with the promise of Paradise with him.

The Love of God embraces all
  whose pride is punctured by the truth.

Seven words
III

In the story of the crucifixion,
Jesus entrusted the beloved disciple
  to his mother,
and her to him.

The Love of God protects intimacy.

Seven words
IV

In the story of the crucifixion,
Jesus shared our terror of abandonment
when he cried out with the question,
Why have you forsaken me?

The Love of God bears the pain.

Seven words
V

In the story of the crucifixion,
Jesus knew the agony of thirst.

The Love of God yearns and groans.

Seven words
VI

In the story of the crucifixion,
Jesus completed his task, crying,
It is finished,
it is fulfilled,
it is done.

The Love of God endures faithfully to the end.

Seven words
VII

In the story of the crucifixion,
Jesus commended his whole being
  to the God from whom he came.

The Love of God trusts that all shall be well.

An eleventh commandment

Thou shalt not kill in the name of any god.

ABOUT THE FONT 'RENARD'

Renard was designed in 1992 by Fred Smeijers, the renowned Dutch typographer, and issued by the Enschedé Font Foundry. Renard is an interpretation of a 2-line Double Pica Roman (Gros Canon) cut by the Flemisch punchcutter Hendrik van den Keere in around 1570, and shown in Plantin's folio specimen of c.1585. Van den Keere's typeface was cut in a large size for display setting: for use in choirbooks for example. Such a book would be placed in front of the choir, so it had to be legible for all the singers in poor lighting conditions. To achieve legibility the typeface is rather condensed, with a large x-height and dark overall colour. Van den Keere never cut a complete italic, so Renard's italic is a new design, made in the spirit of the period.

ABOUT THE PAPER

This book is printed on 120 gsm Corolla Ivory Book Wove, made in Verona, Italy. It is acid-free and made from ecological pulps with low chlorine content, supplied by manufacturers adopting environment-friendly and reforestation policies.